IN THIS SERIES

THE COMPOSITE GUIDE

to **MARTIAL ARTS**

ANN GRAHAM GAINES

CHELSEA HOUSE PUBLISHERS

Philadelphia

Produced by Choptank Syndicate, Inc. and Chestnut Productions

Senior Editor: Norman L. Macht
Editor and Picture Researcher: Mary E. Hull
Design and Production: Lisa Hochstein
Cover Illustrator: Cliff Spohn

Project Editor: Jim McAvoy
Art Direction: Sara Davis
Cover Design: Keith Trego

© 2000 by Chelsea House Publishers,
a subsidiary of Haights Cross Communications.
Printed and bound in the United States of America.

First Printing

1 3 5 7 9 8 6 4 2

Library of Congress Cataloging-in-Publication Data

Gaines, Ann.
    The composite guide to martial arts / by Ann Graham Gaines.
        p. cm.—(The composite guide)
    Includes bibliographical references and index.
    Summary: Provides a historical overview of martial arts, explaining the
various forms of this activity.
    ISBN 0-7910-5866-2
    1. Martial arts—Juvenile literature. [1. Martial arts.] I. Title: Martial arts.
II. Title. III. Series.
GV1101.35. .G35 2000
796.8—dc21
                                                             99-462033

CONTENTS

FIGHTING BULLS WITH EMPTY HANDS

1

Sosai Masutatsu Oyama, one of the greatest martial artists of all time, was born on July 27, 1923, in a village in southern Korea near the Yellow Sea. Mas, as he was known, began his martial arts training at a local elementary school.

Chabee, a Korean form of jiu-jitsu and kempo, was part of the physical education program at Oyama's school. Oyama hated school, but he never missed a chabee lesson. When he was nine he went to live on his sister's farm in Manchuria, where he studied a Chinese form of boxing known as "the Eighteen Hands." Every evening Mas and his father would practice for an hour.

In 1938, Mas went to Japan, where he hoped to become an airplane pilot. He was very poor and had to abandon his desire to fly, but he continued studying all the martial arts that were popular in Japan at the time, especially judo and boxing. One day, Mas met Gishin Funakoshi, a karate master, and became his pupil. By the time Mas was 20, he had become an expert and could easily defeat most opponents at the school. Even though Mas was respected by his teachers and friends, he felt great emptiness. He had not acquired a sense of purpose in his life.

In 1945 Mas met So Nei Chu, a Korean master of goju-ryu karate. This great teacher had a

Today over 10 million people worldwide practice kyokushin karate, a mixture of martial arts disciplines developed by the Korean master Mas Oyama in the 1950s.

profound influence on Mas. During his years of study under So Nei Chu, Mas learned not only a new style of fighting, but a new way of life: the most valuable goals of a student of the martial arts were a peaceful mind and the dedication of one's life to a higher purpose. These attitudes would be the real weapons that led to personal satisfaction.

Once Mas had recognized these as goals to be achieved, he retreated to a remote mountain in Japan to train alone. Beginning in 1946, Mas lived for 14 months in a small hut on the side of Mount Kiyosume, overlooking the Pacific Ocean. Every day he practiced the techniques of karate and meditated to achieve inner peace. In the evening, after fixing himself a simple meal, he would practice playing the flute. When Mas came down from the mountain, he was a different person; he had dedicated his life to the perfection of the martial arts. He could walk on his finger, smash wooden telephone poles, and shatter stones. In 1947, Mas Oyama won the All-Japan Karate Tournament.

In order to demonstrate that his style was superior to all others, Mas Oyama decided to put his skills against 1,200-pound bulls in a small pen. He went from town to town, putting advertisements in the newspapers telling everyone that he would fight a bull with his bare hands. On the appointed day, Mas would stand in a small ring, facing a large, angry bull. He stood silently and still in the center of the ring until the bull became aware of his presence and charged. As the bull lowered his head to catch Mas with a sharp-tipped horn, Oyama turned to one side and chopped off the horn with a single blow of his hand. When the bull turned and charged again, Mas pivoted out of the way and punched the bull in its side as it passed. Three times his blow killed a bull; in more than 50 battles, he always chopped off at least one horn.

Audiences could not believe the awesome power of Mas Oyama as he fought the bulls unarmed. The news of these remarkable bull-fights soon spread around the world. In 1952 he gave his first demonstration in Hawaii, where he met a young student, Bobby Lowe. Oyama invited Lowe to come to Tokyo and train with him. In 1957 Bobby returned to Hawaii and opened the first American kyokushin karate school.

Kyokushin karate is a demanding martial art that teaches students how to smash boards and bricks with a blow of the hand. Showing students how to break a stone is Professor Tatsuo Suzuki, a 7th Dan world karate champion.

Many people wanted to study with Mas. He opened his first karate school, or "Dojo," in 1953. Having studied many different forms of the martial arts—karate, judo, kempo, and others—he took whatever he found to be effective in each and called his style "kyokushin karate." Kyokushin means "the ultimate truth."

In 1954, Mas joined a Japanese karate team for a three-month tournament tour of Southeast Asia. Years earlier, the Japanese had lost an important martial arts tournament to the kickboxers from Thailand. Mas was determined to bring the championship back to Japan. He was scheduled to fight the welterweight champion Black Cobra. Black Cobra was undefeated, and no one thought Oyama could defeat him. Black Cobra struck first, knocking Oyama flat on his back. Oyama jumped right back to his feet, and, with a single blow of his fist, broke Black Cobra's jaw, knocking him unconscious to win the match. Mas went on to defeat all of the Thai boxers. Acknowledged as the best fighter in the world, Mas went on to win over 200 straight matches, fighting experts from many martial arts styles.

Today more than 10 million people around the world are students of kyokushin karate, a demanding sport that includes breaking bricks and thick wooden boards with a blow of the hand. Progress in the sport depends on full-contact matches, although no strikes to the head are allowed. The ultimate test to achieve recognition as a master demands that the student fight 100 opponents in less than four hours. Each bout lasts two minutes. If a pupil is knocked down for more than five seconds, even if it happens in the final fight, he loses. Not only must the student survive the 100 fights, he must win more than half of them.

To show that this feat was not impossible, Mas Oyama once fought 100 opponents on each of three consecutive days. He wanted to continue on the fourth day, but there were no more opponents left to fight. Only 13 other people have ever successfully completed the ordeal of the Hundred Man Kumite, as it is called. It remains the greatest test of physical and mental perseverance in all of the martial arts.

"**M**artial arts" is a term that comes from the Latin language and means the techniques used to become an expert in war or fighting. Since the beginning of human civilization, all societies have taught people how to defend themselves and their families. Human beings have always been aggressive, fighting for scarce food as well as pride and conquest.

More than 6,000 years ago in Egypt, the tombs of the pharaohs were decorated with pictures of boxers facing each other, wearing protective gloves on their fists. Scenes of what look like kickboxing and wrestling appear in the tombs of the Sumerian kings of Mesopotamia from 5,000 years ago. In Asia, the martial arts have also existed since before the beginning of recorded history. As early as 50 B.C., paintings in the tombs of Korean kings showed unarmed combat between men poised to strike from various fighting stances. Throughout Asia, various forms of armed and unarmed combat were developed by the warrior classes and the common people as both military training and self-defense.

In ancient Greece, more than 2,500 years ago, students practiced pankration, a deadly free-for-all fighting technique of boxing and wrestling, in a school called an akademos, from which we get the word academy. These matches were often fought to the death. In order to honor

This statue of the Buddha in meditation was carved in southern India thousands of years ago. The Buddha, a Hindu prince named Siddhartha who attained enlightenment through yoga and meditation, promoted a philosophy of self-improvement that remains the cornerstone of the martial arts.

the best warriors of their society, the Greeks created the Olympic Games in 776 B.C., featuring a single 192-meter race. In 708 B.C., the Greeks added wrestling to the Olympic Games. Olympic wrestling was a brutal affair. One of the most effective moves was to break the fingers of the opponent so that he could not use his hands in the bout. But these wrestling matches were not fought to the death.

Boxing was added to the Olympic Games as another sport 20 years later. Originally boxers could use open-handed blows and kicks, which made the sport look a lot like today's karate or tae kwon do. These early matches had no rules, no time limits, and no scoring. The boxer left standing at the end was the winner.

Combats to the death were continued in Rome during its Imperial Period (approximately 50 B.C. to 400 A.D.) in contests between professional warriors called gladiators, but almost all of the martial arts soon became part of military training or sports in which the athletes did not die.

In Korea and on the island of Okinawa, the kicking and punching arts called tae kwon do and karate were perfected. In Japan, jiu-jitsu, judo, and aikido, all of which use throws and pins, developed. In Thailand, muay Thai, a kick boxing art, was invented. Silat, another martial art that uses the legs to kick and take down an opponent, was developed in Malaysia and Indonesia. Philippine islanders developed a martial art called Escrima, which uses short sticks called bastons to defeat an opponent.

The physical techniques common to all the fighting reached a new level of effectiveness

A 74-year-old Buddhist monk strikes a martial arts pose while exercising at a Shaolin monastery near Zhengzhan, Henan, China. Shaolin monasteries have promoted the martial arts since 600 A.D.

when they combined with an inner, mental training in self-discipline.

About 10,000 years ago, a warrior people from what is now Iran and southern Russia invaded and conquered the vast subcontinent of India. The warrior classes of these Aryans, as they were called, had a system of martial

The art of karate originated as a form of self-defense in ancient Korea and Japan. Demonstrating proper kicking technique, French competitor Corinne Terrine, right, swings her right foot up against Canadian Carole Haddad at the 1999 Ladies Cup Karate Tournament held in Tokyo, Japan.

arts and self-defense much like those developed in the rest of the world.

In addition, the Aryans had a system of practices called yoga, a martial art directed against the internal physical and mental functions of the self. No matter how skilled a soldier was with the sword or the fist, if that soldier was fat or sickly or afraid, he was easily defeated. The priests and ruling classes of the Aryans developed physical and mental exercises designed to improve the students' self-discipline and give them the ability to say no to the many destructive whims and desires that the mind presents to the consciousness of the person. The successful practice of yoga gradually eliminated these destructive impulses from the minds of the warriors and left them calm, healthy, and unafraid to face the challenges of the world around them.

Many centuries passed, and the Aryans, now called Hindus, continued to rule India. Around 563 B.C., a Hindu prince, Siddhartha Gautama, was born in India. He was a sensitive young man who soon became aware that, although he was a prince living in great luxury and could have anything he wanted, almost everyone else lived in great misery. Besides, no matter how rich or powerful a person was, he was not so for long. Death, if not conflict, during a short life would take all possessions and happiness away from everyone, king or slave alike. Siddhartha decided to renounce his princely inheritance and roam the earth in search of a true and permanent peace of mind that conquered the reality of life. For years, he practiced yoga and other forms of self-discipline to purify and calm his mind. Nothing seemed to work; he failed year after year to attain what he called enlightenment.

Siddhartha decided to simply sit silently and unmoving in one place until the answer either came to him or he died. His training in yoga had made his will very strong. Siddhartha was able to focus his attention on nothing at all. Without thought and perfectly determined to achieve his goal, he sat, breathing. It is said that the roots of the plants around him grew as thick as a man's wrist around his body as he sat there under a tree. Finally, one day, Siddhartha Gautama became the Buddha, the enlightened one. He was at peace. Everything became all right; his misery and the misery of all mankind disappeared. He got up and never thought about it again.

For the rest of his life the Buddha roamed throughout India and preached that peace and the perfection of the human spirit lay within the grasp of everyone if they would only search within themselves with the same dedication he had shown. Many people followed the example of the Buddha. His followers are called Buddhists, and they established monasteries throughout Asia where they lived together and searched for their own enlightenment. Many called the Buddha a god or divine, but that was not his doing. Buddhism became a philosophy of self-improvement.

The connection between the martial arts and Buddhism began around 600 A.D., when Bodhidharma, a warrior Buddhist monk from India, traveled to China to inspect the Buddhist Shaolin monastery there. He found the monks at the monastery who were translating Indian Buddhist writings into Chinese to be unhappy, sickly, and not making much progress toward their own enlightenment. Bodhidharma gave the Shaolin community new yoga practices in meditation as well as physical exercises designed to improve the monks' general health. These exercises were called "The Change of the Sinews," "The Marrow Washing," and the "Eighteen Hand Movements." Bodhidharma later devised self-defense movements based on his knowledge of Indian fighting systems. He emphasized the connection between the outer physical martial arts and the inner yogic control achieved through proper breathing. This connection between breathing, meditation, and physical fighting techniques formed the foundation of all the modern martial arts.

The monks of the Shaolin monastery soon became skilled martial artists, famous throughout China for their prowess and courage. From all over China, men were drawn to the Shaolin monastery to learn the new martial arts secrets. In 698 A.D., Emperor T'ai Tsung of the Tang dynasty called upon the fighting monks of Shaolin to aid him in his war against General Wang-Shih-Chung, who had gathered a large army in an attempt to oust the Tang emperor from the throne. A small force of the Shaolin answered this call and were instrumental in the victory of the emperor. A strong bond was developed between the imperial household and the Shaolin monks. Shaolin fighting techniques were taught in the military, and Shaolin monasteries were established in other locations in China.

For over a thousand years, the Shaolin monks taught the basic principle of joining the external, bodily, movements and internal self-discipline and control. Various styles, usually named for animals in nature, such as the tiger or the crane, became popular in the provinces of China, but all of them used the Shaolin techniques.

KUNG FU

The martial arts training that Bodhidharma gave to the Shaolin monks in China drew on traditional Chinese forms of self-defense that were already centuries old at the time. Several hundred years after Bodhidharma died, another monk, Chueh Yuan, revised the works of Bodhidharma and created the "72 Styles of Movements" from the "18 Fists of Lo Han." Over the next 50 years, Chueh Yuan and a Chinese martial artist named Pai Yu-feng revised the Shaolin texts and expanded the 72 styles into 170 techniques. These 170 basic throws, kicks, and holds became the foundation of all the Shaolin martial arts and are called kung fu, which means "skill achieved over time through practice."

As the Shaolin teachings spread, they were adapted to the styles of fighting that were native to the peoples who lived near the Buddhist monasteries. The Chinese martial artists had a saying: "Fists in the south, kicks in the north." Around the year 800 A.D., Shaolin priests opened the Wutang Tiger Temple in northern China, near the border of Manchuria and Korea. They developed a style of kung fu that was based on the kicking systems of self-defense already popular in the region. The northern Shaolin style of kung fu used quick explosive kicks, often delivered in a series of two or three, while jumping into the air. Those who practiced the northern kung fu style would avoid an attack

Kung fu master Shiu Hon-Sang demonstrates a lightning kick to follow up the ending of an aggressive movement. The northern style of Shaolin kung fu is best known for its rapid kicks.

rather than block it and remain at long range from an opponent unless attacking.

A southern style of kung fu used hand techniques like punching, chopping and grabbing. Its practitioners concentrated on a close-range, blocking defense. Hung gar is a style of kung fu that was developed in southern China, stressing close-quarter fighting methods. Powerful boxing blows are delivered from a stationary position called the "horse stance." Hung gar became popular in the cities where most combats took place in narrow alleys and inside buildings. Choy lee fut is another style of kung fu that is based on the closing-in power of the horse stance. Besides using grappling and throwing techniques and high

Chinese girls practice kung fu outdoors. The girl on the right delivers a powerful kick in the northern Shaolin style.

and low kicks, in choy lee fut one tries to over-power an opponent by moving directly into his or her body. Straight punches, hooks, and uppercuts delivered from less than a foot away are used to put the opponent off balance and on the ground.

Many different styles of martial arts developed over the years. There were no rules or laws to stop individuals from inventing and promoting their own system. If a martial artist was successful over a period of time using a particular style of fighting, others would want to learn it.

In 1842, Kau See, a normally peaceful citizen of China, resisted being drafted into the army. He fought and killed the army officer sent to recruit him. For this crime he was sent to prison. He spent 10 years in a cell watching the monkeys who were used as prison guards. The monkeys would howl and attack anyone who escaped from their cages. They made cheap and effective prison guards. Kau See watched them and saw how they fought among themselves. After he was released, he developed an effective style of kung fu that was based on the hopping and squatting defenses of the monkeys. He became known as "Monkey Master" and attracted many followers. Monkey kung fu is still practiced in China.

In addition to the monkey, the natural movements of other animals were used as the basis of new kung fu styles. About 300 years ago, Wang Lang founded the praying mantis form of kung fu. He watched and admired the ability of the insect, which remains calm for long periods while hunting for food and then strikes quickly and with deadly force at the most vital points of the nearby meal. Wang copied the body positions of the mantis as well as its methods of attack and formed a very effective style of fighting. He soon had many pupils. After his death, four of his pupils each claimed that they had invented even more effective strikes. They agreed to name their styles after the markings on the backs of praying mantises they captured. Thus, the plum blossom, seven stars, bare, and yin-yang styles of praying mantis kung fu were invented. Hundreds of different styles of kung fu have come into existence. Many are popular for a time and then disappear, often to reappear decades later with a slightly different name. Several of the animal forms of kung fu have lasted for centuries. The white crane, the leopard, the tiger, the snake, and the dragon are all long-lived combat styles that use their namesake animals as the basis of their effectiveness. All of these have a long history of masters and pupils and continue to be popular today. And all of these styles have roots in the Shaolin practice of combining exercises for the mind and the body.

Kung fu was the first Asian martial art to become widely practiced in the United States. Television and movies made kung fu popular during the 1970s. The person most responsible for this popularity was Bruce Lee, born Lee Jun Fan in San Francisco, California, on November 27, 1940. His family soon returned to Hong Kong, an island off the southern coast of China, where Bruce grew up and studied martial arts with his father.

The kung fu that Bruce learned was called wing chun, a style based on the idea of waiting

Bruce Lee demonstrates a kung fu leap and kick on the set of The Chinese Connection. *Lee, best known for his 1973 film* Enter the Dragon, *brought kung fu to American audiences.*

for the first strike of an opponent. Its practitioners always want to be the defender, never the aggressor. Once an opponent launches the first strike, the defender absorbs and neutralizes the strike. At this point, the attacker is extended beyond his natural defenses and is vulnerable to a counterattack, which is delivered with a penetrating thrust. This close-in style of southern kung fu is popular in Hong Kong.

Between 1954 and 1959, Lee studied wing chun under masters named Yip Man, Wong Shun-Leung, and William Cheung. Bruce was not only an expert martial artist by this time, he was also handsome, charming, hardworking, and an excellent dancer, winning the Hong Kong Crown Colony Cha-Cha Contest in 1958.

Bruce Lee, right, starred with Van Williams in the 1960s adventure television show The Green Hornet. *Lee's character, Kato, introduced kung fu to American audiences.*

Bruce Lee returned to the United States in April 1959. After legally changing his name to Bruce Lee, he settled in Seattle, Washington, and gave demonstrations of kung fu to college students and others interested in the martial arts. In 1963, he wrote a book on kung fu called *Chinese Gung Fu: The Philosophical Art of Self Defense.* Although the book was popular among those already interested in the martial arts, it was a television show that first made Bruce Lee and kung fu popular with most young Americans. From September 1966 to July 1967, Bruce appeared as Kato, the kung fu hero in the television show *The Green Hornet*, which was based on a popular comic book. The show was not a success, but his explosive, high flying martial arts moves made Bruce a TV star.

Lee later starred in a series of Hollywood martial arts movies that became super box office successes, including *Enter the Dragon* and *Return of the Dragon*, both released in 1973. Soon there were many imitators of these fast-moving and exciting movies, and all of the Asian martial arts achieved a popularity they had never before realized.

Bruce Lee died of a cerebral edema in 1973 and, though he is remembered today as a movie star, his dedication to the spirit of the martial arts is often overlooked.

4   JIU-JITSU AND JUDO

Of all the countries in the Orient, Japan prized the arts of war the most. Beginning in the 13th century, the chiefs of Japan's districts fought constantly among themselves to rule the entire island. These chiefs taught some subjects to become warriors, or samurai, and elevated them above the rest of the villagers. The samurai—"one who serves"—trained in kendo, the art of swords, and kyudo, the art of the bow and arrow.

In case a samurai was ever caught without his swords on the battlefield, he also trained in jiu-jitsu, which means "the gentle way." Jiu-jitsu used throws and holds that enabled an unarmed warrior to put his opponent on the ground, where he could be killed with a strangle hold, a knife, a stick, or even a paper fan—in other words, anything that the warrior could grab.

The Edo Era in Japan, 1603–1867, was considered to be the high point of the samurai culture, in which flower arranging and poetry writing, as well as the martial arts of the sword and jiu-jitsu, were practiced by male members of the upper classes of Japan. Japan and its samurai culture suffered a great humiliation in the 1860s when the more technologically advanced lands of the United States and Europe forced Japan to accept foreign merchants in their country. The Japanese decided that their

Ylenia Scapian of Italy, right, and Tetyana Beliaeve of the Ukraine compete in the women's 72 kg. judo quarterfinal at the 1996 Olympics in Atlanta, Georgia. Creating imbalance in one's opponent is one of the objects of judo.

nation had to become the equal of the Western powers in order to regain its national honor. Japan then outlawed the samurai warriors and established a modern army with guns. The art of jiu-jitsu was taught only as physical exercise in schools and the army.

Kano Sensei was a physical education instructor who changed jiu-jitsu to a less dangerous sport. He called his sport "judo," which, like jiu-jitsu, means "the gentle way," and he eliminated the use of weapons. He also stopped teaching moves that could be instantly fatal to an opponent. Using leverage and an opponent's momentum to throw him to the ground and hold him immobile, he based the new martial art on the idea of maximum efficiency with minimum effort.

Judo, as it evolved, is not an especially violent art, but it is certainly rough-and-tumble. It is necessary to be in top physical condition to perform well. For this reason, judo continued to be part of physical training in the armed forces around the world and especially in Japan. Kano Sensei traveled the world for more than 50 years teaching judo before he died in 1938. Martial arts were banned in Japan after the end of World War II, but judo continued to be practiced as a sport in special judo schools called "dojos." The ban was later lifted. Today, judo is recognized as a sport that encourages skill, self-discipline, and health. Judo became the first Asian martial art to become an Olympic sport in 1964.

Just as in the regular school system, progress in judo is marked by different grades. What grade a student of judo, or "judoka," has reached is shown by the color of the belt he or she wears with the white judo uniform, or "judogi." A newcomer to the sport wears a plain white belt, followed by yellow, orange, green, blue, and brown belts that are won as the student becomes better. The next level of judo is a master, or "dan," who is authorized to wear a black belt.

To achieve each level, a student must pass an examination and win matches with others who want to achieve that higher level. A fifth-degree dan is the highest black belt awarded for competitive excellence. There are 10 levels of black belt in all. The final five levels can be awarded only by an examination in Japan and

Masayuki Hasimoto throws an opponent in a judo match at the Baltimore YMCA. According to the code of judo, an opponent must surrender gracefully when he has been thrown and immobilized. The pinned wrestler acknowledges his submission by patting or lightly hitting the floor or his opponent's body with his hand or foot.

A judoist flips his opponent over his head during a practice session. Quick movement and leverage are the essence of judo, which evolved from jiu-jitsu.

go only to people who have contributed to the sport outside of competition. Only seven men have ever been awarded the 10th-degree black belt.

Each beginning student of judo is first taught how to fall or be thrown without injury. Students are taught to fall forward, backward, and how to feel comfortable upside down. This skill, called "ukemi," is the basis for all that will come after. Next the student is introduced to "nagewaza," or throwing techniques, and "katamewaza," or techniques on the ground. There are not many techniques, so the basic moves of judo are easily learned.

The successful moves in judo are based on three principles: balance (kuzushi), posture (tsukuri), and the throw (kake). It is necessary to keep your own balance at all times while creating an imbalance in your opponent. Both of these are needed to take the opponent to the mat under control. Balance is a result of proper body postures. These simple postures can be learned easily and perfected with practice. It is not the number of fantastic moves that makes a good judoist but the fluid quickness of mind and body working together that can change an opponent's moves into an advantage. Judo is not a sport of simple strength but a sport of simple moves and a calm, quick mind.

Perhaps the greatest judo master of all time is Yasuhiro Yamashita. Born in Kumamoto, Japan, on July 1, 1957, he started learning judo when he was in the third grade. As a child, he was an overweight brat. His parents thought some judo training would help him lose a few pounds and help with his attitude problem. It fixed his attitude, but he never lost any weight.

"When I was young there were times when I hit somebody or punched them," he recalled, "But I was told if I carried on this way, I would have to leave judo. So I changed my ways," Yamashita has said.

By the time he reached junior high school, he had already been awarded a black belt for his superior achievements in the sport. In 1977, Yamashita became the All-Japan champion, the youngest champion in the history of the sport. He went on to win nine All-Japan Championships and four World Championships in a row.

At the 1984 Olympic Games in Los Angeles, California, the 280-pound Yasuhiro came into the competition with 194 consecutive victories. He had not been beaten in seven years, since the year he won his first All-Japan title. He was not only huge, but possessed lightning speed. In the Olympic competition, he won his first match in just 12 seconds. In his second match, against Arthur Schnabel of France, Yasuhiro suffered a torn calf muscle. Despite the painful injury, he got Schnabel in a choke hold and ended the match in three minutes. In the gold medal match, the hobbled Japanese star sidestepped a move by Mohamed Rashwan of Egypt, tripped, and fell on him for a win just 65 seconds into the match. When Yasuhiro

Natik Bagirov of Belarus, right, squeezes Germany's Richard Trautmann in a judo hold during the men's lightweight judo competition at the 1996 Olympics.

returned to Japan he was awarded a sixth-degree black belt and became a Judoist of the Sixth Dan, achieving one of the highest honors that anyone can attain in the sport. The nation of Japan proclaimed him a national hero.

In April 1985, Yamashita retired from active competition after 14 years of competition and a record of 203 consecutive victories. "It was a long time," he said. "I was getting tired of the top level competition. I had had enough."

In all of that time Yamashita never used his skills outside of the ring. "Judo is training not only a person's body but his heart and his feelings. A really strong person never shows that kind of behavior. Sometimes there are strong people who do that but their heart is not good."

Since 1988, Yamashita has held positions as an assistant professor at Takai University and as the head coach of the Japan Judo League.

TAE KWON DO

In the ancient kingdom of Koguryo on the Korean peninsula, the rulers believed that the hands were only to be used for positive artistic endeavors like writing poetry and drawing pictures. The feet were the proper body parts to be used for self-defense. Thus they developed an effective self-defense called sobak that combined Chinese and Mongolian kicking techniques.

In those days, the Korean peninsula was divided into three kingdoms: Koguryo in the north, Paekche, and Silla in the south. The kingdom of Silla was constantly attacked by pirates and Japanese raiders. Gwahggaeto, the king of Koguryo, sent armed forces to help his neighboring kingdom fight the pirates. These allies passed the secrets of their martial art to the warrior class of Silla, who called it taek kyon. The Silla warriors, known as the Hwarang, established a military academy that taught taek kyon as part of the general education of their kingdom's youth. The principles of the academy were loyalty, obedience, trustworthiness, valor in battle, and respect for human life. These qualities became linked with the aims of taek kyon.

Throughout history, the Korean peninsula has undergone many changes and seen many different kingdoms and invaders, including the Chinese and the Japanese. Regardless of who ruled, taek kyon continued to be taught, often in secret, by masters of the art.

The U.S.A.'s Mark Lopez, right, fights South Korea's Dae-Hyu Ko at the 1999 World Tae Kwon Do Championships in Edmonton, Alberta, Canada. Tae Kwon Do contestants protect themselves by wearing a body pad known as a hoogoo, as well as a helmet.

Following the expulsion of the Japanese, who had ruled Korea from 1909 to 1945, the Korean national martial arts underwent an explosion in popularity. Within a year, three separate schools for martial arts opened in Seoul alone. In the next decade, seven other schools opened. Each of these schools claimed to teach the true Korean national martial art, but each was slightly different from the others, and each had a slightly different name, like soo bahk do, kwon bop, kong soo do, tae soo do or dang soo do. In order to establish rules and competitions for all, the masters of these schools met. On April 11, 1955, they decided to unite under the name of tae kwon do, which means "the way of the hand and the foot," or "the art of kicking and punching." Tae kwon do also means "the art of unarmed combat." No weapons are used in tae kwon do. A competitor attacks his opponent with bare hands and feet.

One of the best and most famous masters of Korean tae kwon do is not a Korean but an American, Chuck Norris, the television and movie star. In his television show, *Walker, Texas Ranger*, Norris plays a rough-and-ready hero, a Texas Ranger who is always ready to fight six or eight bad guys. In the movies, Norris starred in several successful martial arts action features like *Return of the Dragon*, released in 1973, and *Game of Death* in 1978. Not many people know that Chuck Norris was also a seven-time world middleweight karate champion.

Norris was born Carlos Ray Norris on March 10, 1940, in Ryan, Oklahoma, the oldest of three boys in a family led by his mother.

It was up to Chuck and his mom to take care of everybody and put food on the family table. The family moved 16 times by the time Chuck was 10 years old. As a boy, he dreamed of becoming a police officer. After high school graduation, he joined the United States Air Force and spent four years in the military police in Korea.

Norris started studying judo as a part of his military training. When he visited the local villages, he saw a new kind of self-defense training that amazed him: Korean youths combating an attacker not with holds or throws but with jump-spinning kicks in the air. "I couldn't believe a human body could do all of those things: jumps, heel kicks, and all that. And they looked so mean, I was afraid to go over and ask what they were doing." Norris learned that what he saw was called tae kwon do. He went to a local master, Mr. Shin, and convinced him to take on another pupil.

Ray Murphy, 66, deflects the kicks of his grandsons Kevin, 15, left, and Scott, 12, as they demonstrate tae kwon do moves. The most popular martial art in the world, tae kwon do is practiced by people of all ages worldwide.

Tae kwon do teaches a variety of kicking techniques. First, students learn to make kicks with the ball, heel, and instep of the foot from both standing and kneeling positions. Kicks go to the front, back, and sides of the body. Once the students have perfected these basic kicking moves, they are taught to deliver them while turning and jumping in the air. Students are trained to improve their jumps by jumping from the floor onto a box, and then over the box. When the student can deliver the kicks while jumping over the box, a bigger box is used for practice. Soon the best student can easily jump several feet into the air and deliver a variety of spinning kicks.

Chuck trained day and night, five hours a day, six days a week. On Sundays, he practiced judo. By the time he left Korea, he had a black belt in tae kwon do and a brown belt in judo. The martial arts training had a profound influence on his character. "When I was growing up," Norris recalled, "I was a real shy kid. I guess not having a father image, a man to give you that strength of character, contributed to that. Martial arts really changed all that. That's why I'm such an advocate of the martial arts—because it does help you change your life in a positive direction. It helps you to be able to communicate, to be more self-assured, and it raises your self-esteem, which is the most important thing. It instills discipline and respect, which is lacking in many young kids. Discipline was the most important lesson I learned very early on in my martial arts career."

In 1966, Norris won the All-American Karate Championship in New York and the

International Karate Middleweight Championship. The next year, he again won the Middleweight Championship and added the Grand Championship by defeating both the lightweight and heavyweight champions as well. He repeated as the grand champion in 1968. That year he also won the international world middleweight title and then held it undefeated until the end of his competitive career in 1974.

Norris became a champion in karate, a martial art very similar to tae kwon do, because, at the time, there were no international competitions in tae kwon do. The World Tae Kwon Do Federation was formed in 1973 and has conducted international level competitions since then. The United States Tae Kwon Do Union (USTU), established in 1974, became the national governing body for tae kwon do in the United States in 1984. The USTU organizes national events like the U.S. Open Tae Kwon Do Championships and the U.S. Olympic team trials.

The martial arts of Asia were relatively unknown in the United States and Europe in the 1970s, when Chuck Norris was the world karate champion. There was not much money to be made in karate, and he found it hard to support his own family, which by then included two children. At the time, he was giving martial arts lessons to movie stars in Hollywood. They convinced him to try out for a small part in the martial arts movie *Return of the Dragon*, starring the young and handsome kung fu master, Bruce Lee. The movie was a great success among young people and gave Norris an idea. He decided to make his own martial arts movie.

"I went around and met with potential investors and told them that there were about four million karate people in the world, and that I was the world champion for six years and they couldn't see me fight anymore because I was retired, so the only way they could see me fight now is on-screen. I said, if only half of them go, you've got a $6 million gross on your investment. So I got the money to make the movie."

Norris' 1979 film *Good Guys Wear Black* made $18 million in the United States alone and turned him into a movie star. He followed with more popular and successful martial arts movies, including the *Missing in Action* trilogy. *Walker, Texas Ranger* is seen regularly by millions of viewers, many of whom now study tae kwon do.

In 1996 Norris was awarded an 8th-degree black belt in tae kwon do, and he is one of only a handful of westerners ever to receive that honor.

In 1990 Norris founded Kick Drugs Out of America, a foundation dedicated to fighting the war on drugs and stopping youth violence. Kick Drugs Out of America teaches school children karate as part of their daily school curriculum, offering them a chance to learn the martial arts disciplines and to gain self-confidence and self-esteem. By 2000 more than 4,000 school kids participated in the program, which was shown to increase self-discipline and school attendance rates.

Tae kwon do was a demonstration sport at the 1988 Olympic Games held in Seoul, South Korea, and the 1992 Games in Barcelona, Spain. Tae kwon do contests were not held at the 1996 Olympic Games due to the International Olympic Committee's decision to eliminate demonstration sports from the Games.

Contestants are protected by a heavy uniform called a hoogoo and a face guard. Matches are conducted in three three-minute rounds and are judged by five judges positioned around the seven-meter square ring.

The first person to win an Olympic medal in tae kwon do was a woman, Arlene Limas from the United States. Limas won the gold medal in the women's heavyweight sparring division.

In the year 2000 tae kwon do made its debut as an official Olympic sport at the Games held in Sydney, Australia. Tae kwon do is officially practiced in over 120 countries of the world today by more than 20 million people. It is the most popular martial art in the world.

Morihei Ueshiba was born in the small fishing village of Tanabe, Japan, on December 14, 1883. After three daughters, his parents welcomed their new son with great joy. Ueshiba, who had been born prematurely, was pampered by everyone in the family as he grew up. He started to go to the Shigon Buddhist temple in his neighborhood at an early age. Shigon Buddhism teaches that it is possible for each person to attain perfect happiness and tranquility during their lives through their own efforts and for all of humanity to bring that perfect peace to reality on earth.

The search for achieving that perfection for all men became the driving force in the life of Ueshiba. He began to study various forms of martial arts as a teenager. From the beginning of his training, he recognized that a true martial artist must train his mind as well as his body. He became an expert in jiu-jitsu and ken-jitsu, the art of the sword. He tried to enlist in the army but was refused because he was barely five feet tall, two inches below the minimum height. For a year, he ran everyday to the secluded mountains near his home. There he would hang himself from a tree with weights tied to his feet in order to stretch his spine and become taller. He finally passed the army physical and served in the Japanese army during the Russo-Japanese War. Disturbed by the horrors of that bloody

An aikido competitor uses his energy to reroute the force of an attacker, causing the attacker to fall.

Competitors demonstrate the Japanese martial art of aikido, which teaches practitioners to redirect the force of an opponent to their advantage.

war, he returned to civilian life in 1908 and dedicated his life to the martial arts and world peace. Around 1915, Ueshiba met two men, Takeda Sokaku and Deguchi Onisaburo, who would direct his path toward those goals.

Takeda Sokaku, who had been born in 1860, was, like Ueshiba, a tiny man, just five feet tall. Sokaku was unable to read or write, but he was a ferocious master of many different martial arts. Like a hired gunfighter in the old days of the American West, Sokaku would travel from province to province and kill the thieves and murderers who infested the countryside. He would often single-handedly fight and kill entire gangs of outlaws. When Sokaku easily defeated Ueshiba in a public contest, Ueshiba immediately asked to become his pupil.

For four years, Ueshiba served as Sokaku's personal servant in exchange for lessons in the martial arts. Sokaku was an extraordinary warrior, but he was suspicious, vain, and afraid of the ghosts of all the men he had killed. Ueshiba wanted more from his life than to be simply a fearful destroyer. Ueshiba became an accomplished master of the martial arts under this teacher, but he eventually left him.

Deguchi Onisaburo was a dreamer, a poet, and a self-proclaimed prophet. He proclaimed in lectures and his daily newspaper that the gods had directed him to bring peace to the world. Millions of Japanese became followers of Omoto-kyo, the name of Deguchi's religion. When Ueshiba met Deguchi in 1919, Deguchi told him that he had had a vision that Ueshiba's father had died. When Ueshiba found out that Deguchi had spoken the truth, Ueshiba immediately became a follower and bodyguard for the religious leader.

Deguchi's vision of world peace reached out to all the world and included all men, but he had little common sense and was easily misled in his grand schemes for a world government. Once Deguchi and Ueshiba traveled to Mongolia and China to establish a new government, but they were quickly arrested by the real Chinese government, who put them in chains and accused them of being Japanese spies. They were soon released and returned to Japan. It was, of course, a foolish plan of dreamers and had no chance of being successful. But it did not seem a foolish plan to Ueshiba, who always gave everything he had to whatever he was doing. He believed with all his might in the goodness of perfect peace and the ability of martial arts training to help him achieve it.

One day in 1925, Ueshiba had a spiritual vision of his own. He saw the universe and everyone and everything within it as one spirit called "Ki." All of the bodies and everything within the universe were to him just parts of the whole. When a person was involved in a conflict, the harmony of the Ki was disturbed. Ueshiba came to view martial arts as a way of training the body to instinctively know how to reestablish the harmony of Ki and to do so quickly and without thought. Ueshiba put all of this philosophy and training into a new discipline which he later called aikido, meaning "the path of the union of breath and energy."

Ueshiba had never stopped the harsh training regimen he had established with Takeda Sokaku, but he suddenly reached a level of mastery never before seen in the martial arts. He could leap over an attacker, he could dodge bullets fired at him, and he could pick up and throw huge boulders. He laughingly defeated any and all martial arts masters who challenged him. They could not harm him, or they fell down trying.

Ueshiba opened his school of aikido in April 1931 and soon had many students.

Many women became his pupils, as well as some of the fiercest masters of karate and judo. Ueshiba lived to be a very old man, almost 86 years old when he died on April 26, 1969. He continued to train and give lessons until the very end. On his deathbed, four of his disciples rushed to his aid when he moaned in pain. He threw all four of them to the floor from his position on his back.

Aikido teaches that attacks are not stopped but are allowed to continue. The body movement of the defender is aligned with the force of the attacker so that the defender becomes the guiding intelligence behind the force of both the attacker and the defender. In this way the force of the attack can be directed into a harmless movement for both. Most attacks are blows or kicks that are directed in a straight line toward the target. Aikido teaches the defender to meet this straight line attack and simply redirect, not stop, its force by the use of a circular movement, in much the same way that a blow to a spinning top is thrown off. The harder the original straight line blow, the harder and farther it is thrown off target. It is the force of the attacker that determines the force of the defense.

It is not that aikido teaches one to be passive in the face of an attack. The defender must be calm and centered in his own mind and body so that he can correctly see the direction and force of the blow without fear and anger clouding the mind or the adrenaline or other chemical reactions to stress making the body tense and off balance. A calm and centered mind in a well-trained body will automatically and without thought protect the defender and the attacker from harm. Aikido is truly a martial art, an outpouring of positive energy that simply swallows the negative energy of an angry attack. With the proper knowledge, women and even children are more than a match for any brute strength.

There are over 700 moves taught in Aikido, divided into two major categories: throwing techniques called "nage waza" and controlling techniques called "katame waza." Aikido-ka, those who practice aikido, also meditate as a part of their training. Learning to exist in a state without thought or awareness of feelings is the goal of meditation. A person who is not concerned with himself in thought and feelings can be instantly aware of the movements and intentions of others. It is only from this state that the aikido-ka has the necessary time to apply the techniques to redirect an attack.

Many people find it hard to stop the mind and body from thinking about itself. One of the techniques used to help a student meditate successfully is breathing correctly and deeply. Students are taught to be aware of how and for how long the breath is drawn into the body, how long it is held inside, and how the breath is expelled from the body. An untrained person breathes about 20 times a minute. Someone who meditates while performing breathing exercises will breathe six to 10 times a minute. Regular deep breathing refreshes the body; combined with a calm and empty mind, it enables the aikido-ka to use his techniques instantly in response to moves, and even thoughts, in truly remarkable ways.

Koichi Tohei, one of the greatest masters of aikido, advises his students that the human body tires quickly when it is constantly tensed but remains fresh and vigorous when relaxed. A newborn baby's body is always soft. Increasing rigidity is a process of passing age.

By insisting that the student practice to strengthen the mind, the spirit, and the body, aikido crosses the line beyond a sport or a martial art into the realm of a philosophy or a way of life. In this way, aikido proves valuable to those who study it, even if they never confront hostility or anger in others. It combines insights into physics and bodily movements with a deep awareness of the spiritual and mental makeup of human beings that brings peace and health.

7 THE MARTIAL ARTS

When someone begins the study of martial arts, it is often because of a humiliation suffered at the hands of a bully. Visions of swiftly defeating a hated opponent give new students the willpower and determination to practice again and again the movements and strikes that will enable them to conquer their oppressors. At a certain point in martial arts training, many students will achieve the same technical, physical mastery of the art. At that point, the one with the calmest mind and the quickest wit is likely to win an encounter.

The Asian martial arts, because of their connection with Buddhist philosophy, calm the mind and quicken the wit if the student is prepared to become even more deeply involved, dedicating years to the study. But even the most accomplished martial artist stands little chance of survival if his opponent is holding a gun and intent on harming him from 20 feet away. The greatest martial artists suggest running away from such a situation if at all possible.

Musashi Miyamoto (1584–1645) was one of the most famous martial artists in the history of Japan. At the age of 50, after winning more than 60 battles, he declared that the real meaning and purpose of the martial arts was to "win without fighting." How can the greatest masters run away from a fight and still claim to be masters?

A Hong Kong resident practices the ancient art of tai chi chuan, also known as Chinese shadowboxing. Tai chi's slow flowing movements appear deceptively simple, but it takes years of practice to perfect the 108 movements.

Why should one devote one's life to such a limited means of defense?

One day, a student of aikido who had recently won his black belt was riding in a subway car in Tokyo when there was a loud commotion at one end of the car. It seemed that a bully was shouting at the passengers, spitting on them, and pushing them around. He was obviously drunk and threatened to hurt the many people who were crowded into the car. The student thought that now would be his chance to demonstrate the many techniques he had learned to defeat such rude and threatening people. It would be a noble gesture on his part to save these people from harm.

The aikido student waited patiently for the bully, who was making his way through the subway car, to reach him. Everyone was silent and obviously afraid of the bully as he approached. Suddenly, there was a small clucking sound from one side of the car, coming from a tiny, ancient man. It got the attention of the bully, who approached the old man. With complete and sincere sympathy and concern, the old man asked the bully to sit down and tell him what made him so troubled. The bully sat down and soon was crying and pouring out his heart about the troubles he was having at home, at his job, and with his ungrateful children. It was over: the danger had passed.

The young man recognized the old man as Morihei Ueshiba, the greatest of them all, fully capable at 80 years old of killing the bully with a single blow. The young student was happy that he could leave the train unnoticed. It was fear that still hid in the remote reaches of the

new black belt's heart that had made him think of physically hurting the bully. It was the complete knowledge of his mastery that had given Ueshiba the calmness to see another way of winning where no one was hurt and where no one lost.

Every morning, millions of people around the world, old and young, greet the new day with what looks like a slow, moving, gentle dance. The dance is made up of a series of body postures that flow together in a sequence called a form. These postures are derived from natural events and have beautiful sounding names such as "crane spreads its wings" or "parting the horse's mane." The entire form,

Ten thousand people gather in Tiananmen Square in Beijing, China, to practice tai chi, which is recognized as a national exercise in China.

when completed, stretches and flexes the body. The rhythmic and peaceful attention required to perform tai chi chuan brings a calm, peaceful state of mind. Although the movements between the various postures appear simple at first, it takes a lifetime of practice to master the smooth flow of energy of the tai chi dance.

Tai chi is like a moving form of yoga, combined with meditation. By concentrating on executing the precise movements, practicers of tai chi clear and calm their minds. Tai chi is recommended as a means of stress management, relaxation, and posture correction. It is also a method of focusing one's energy positively. Like the Chinese tradition of acupuncture, the practice of tai chi is believed to enhance the circulation of "chi," or vital force, within the body.

Tai chi chuan, which means "the grand ultimate truth," was invented as a martial art by a Chinese monk named Zhang San Feng, after watching a struggle between a crane and a snake. He observed how the relaxed circular movements of the snake avoided the quick thrusts of the crane's sharp beak, and imitated these and other movements that he noticed animals using to avoid conflict or attack opponents.

At first tai chi concentrated on the more martial uses of its forms, but tai chi is basically a martial art without an opponent. It is an art for those masters who find that they, themselves, are the only stumbling block to happiness and fulfillment.

Kung fu, tai chi, and other martial arts have been blended into many variations, but they share a common set of values: self confidence, strength, health, and peace of mind. These were the benefits that Bodhidharma envisioned almost 1,400 years ago when he first brought the martial arts to China. They remain the attainable goals for all martial arts students today.

CHRONOLOGY

4000 B.C.	First paintings of martial artists appear in royal tombs in Egypt.
708 B.C.	Wrestling is included in the Greek Olympic Games.
648 B.C.	Pankration, a kind of martial arts boxing, is included in the Greek Olympic Games.
563 B.C.	Siddhartha Gautama, the Buddha, is born in India.
600 A.D.	Bodhidharma, the Indian monk, visits a Chinese Shaolin Buddhist monastery and promotes the martial arts.
700	Shaolin martial artists become allies of the ruling Chinese dynasty.
700-1700	Chinese Shaolin martial arts grow into numerous styles in all parts of Asia.
1200	Chinese Buddhism and Shaolin martial arts are introduced into Japan.
1860-1945	Japanese martial arts are introduced into Korea and Okinawa.
1882	Judo's first training center in Japan opens.
1921	Gichin Funakoshi gives a karate demonstration to the Japanese government.
1925	Morihei Ueshiba invents aikido, using principles of nonviolence.
1945	The end of World War II promotes martial arts participation in Japan.
1964	Judo becomes an Olympic sport at the Games in Tokyo.
1973	The World Tae Kwan Do Federation is formed; Bruce Lee's movies popularize kung fu in the United States.
1988	Tae kwan do becomes a demonstration sport at the Seoul, South Korea, Olympics.
2000	Tae kwan do becomes an official Olympic sport at the Sydney, Australia, Games.

GLOSSARY

Aikido
Japanese martial art, meaning "way of the harmonious spirit" or "the path of the union of breath and energy."

Bodhidharma
Indian monk who brought Buddhist forms of martial arts to Asia.

Chi
Chinese word for the life energy that can be directed by martial arts practice.

Dan
Japanese word for the level of black belt attained, one through 10.

Dojo
Training hall for martial arts.

Gi
Uniform worn to practice martial arts.

Jiu-jitsu
Japanese martial art similar to judo but more dangerous; the word means "gentle way."

Judo
Japanese martial art of throws and holds similar to wrestling.

Karate
Okinawan martial art of strikes and kicks which means "empty hand."

Kata
Japanese word to describe a pattern of exercise in karate.

Kendo
Japanese martial art of the sword.

Ki
Japanese word for the life energy that can be directed by martial arts practice.

Kumite
Japanese karate word for sparring matches.

Kung fu
Chinese martial art, meaning "skill achieved over time through practice."

Kyu
Japanese word for ranks below a black belt.

Kyudu
Japanese martial art of archery.

Muay Thai
Form of kickboxing that comes from Thailand.

Obi
Japanese word for the belt worn with the gi or uniform.

Pankration
Ancient Greek martial art of boxing and wrestling.

Rei
Customary bow; the word also means "respect" and "courtesy" in Japanese.

Samurai
"One who serves" in Japanese, the warrior feudal class in Japan.

Shaolin
An order of Chinese monks who first developed Chinese martial arts.

Sensei
"Teacher" or "master" in Japanese.

Tai chi chuan
Chinese dance or martial art directed at the self.

Tae kwon do
Korean martial art similar to karate, using many jumps and kicks.

Yabusume
Japanese martial art of archery on horseback.

FURTHER READING

Borkowski, Cezar, and Marion Manzo. *The Complete Idiot's Guide to Martial Arts*. Scarborough, Ontario: Prentice Hall Canada, Inc., 1999.

Lee, Bruce. *The Tao of Kung Fu*. Boston: Charles E. Tuttle Co., 1997.

McFarlane, Stewart. *The Complete Book of Tai Chi*. New York: DK Publishing, 1997.

Oyama, Masutatsu. *This Is Karate*. Tokyo: Japan Publications, 1980.

Park, Yeon Hee. *Tae Kwon Do: The Ultimate Reference Guide to the World's Most Popular Martial Art*. New York: Facts On File, 1999.

Reay, Tony and Geoffrey Hobbs. *The Illustrated Guide to Judo*. New York: Van Nostrand Reinhold Company, 1979.

Stevens, John. *Abundant Peace: The Biography of Morihei Ueshiba, Founder of Aikido*. Boston: Shambala, 1987.

Yamada, Yoshimitsu. *The New Aikido Complete: The Arts of Power and Movement*. Seacaucus, New Jersey: Lyle Stuart, Inc., 1981.

INDEX

ANN GRAHAM GAINES has been a freelance writer for 15 years. She lives in the woods near Gonzales, Texas, with her family. She especially enjoys writing books that interest her four children.